SOUND

SOUND

EDITED BY SHERMAN HOLLAR

Britannica
Educational Publishing

IN ASSOCIATION WITH

ROSEN
EDUCATIONAL SERVICES

Published in 2013 by Britannica Educational Publishing
(a trademark of Encyclopædia Britannica, Inc.) in association with Rosen Educational Services, LLC
29 East 21st Street, New York, NY 10010.

Distributed exclusively by Rosen Educational Services.
For a listing of additional Britannica Educational Publishing titles, call toll free (800) 237-9932.

First Edition

Britannica Educational Publishing
J.E. Luebering: Director, Core Reference Group, Encyclopædia Britannica
Adam Augustyn: Assistant Manager, Encyclopædia Britannica

Anthony L. Green: Editor, Compton's by Britannica
Michael Anderson: Senior Editor, Compton's by Britannica
Andrea R. Field: Senior Editor, Compton's by Britannica
Sherman Hollar: SeniorEditor, Compton's by Britannica

Marilyn L. Barton: Senior Coordinator, Production Control
Steven Bosco: Director, Editorial Technologies
Lisa S. Braucher: Senior Producer and Data Editor
Yvette Charboneau: Senior Copy Editor
Kathy Nakamura: Manager, Media Acquisition

Rosen Educational Services
Jeanne Nagle: Senior Editor
Nelson Sá: Art Director
Cindy Reiman: Photography Manager
Karen Huang: Photo Researcher
Brian Garvey: Designer, Cover Design
Introduction by Jeanne Nagle

Library of Congress Cataloging-in-Publication Data

Sound/edited by Sherman Hollar.
    p. cm.—(Introduction to physics)
"In association with Britannica Educational Publishing, Rosen Educational Services."
Audience: 7 to 8
Includes bibliographical references and index.
ISBN 978-1-61530-841-5 (lib. bdg.)
1. Sound—Juvenile literature. I. Hollar, Sherman.
QC225.5.S664 2013
534—dc23

                                                                            2012010563

Manufactured in the United States of America

On the cover, p.3: A hand fingering the fretboard of an electric guitar. The position and pressure of
fingers on the fret determines the tone and pitch of the sound made. © *iStockphoto.com/Anthony Brown*

Cover (equations) © iStockphoto.com/James Thew; pp. 10, 20, 35, 54, 67, 69, 72, 76, 77 Kanwarjit Singh
Boparai/Shutterstock.com; pp. 17, 24, 25, 46, 62, 63, 64 © iStockphoto.com/CWLawrence, remaining
interior background image Yakobchuk Vasyl/Shutterstock.com

CONTENTS

Sound can mean different things to different people, depending on the situation. For instance, a train whistle might let an excited traveler at a railway station know he or she is about to leave on a long-awaited trip. For someone walking near train tracks, however, that same whistle serves as a warning that an engine is coming and the person needs to get out of its path. Likewise, a dog barking at night might make the pooch's owner feel safe from burglars, but may simply annoy neighbors trying to sleep.

Regardless of the situation or interpretation, all sounds have things in common, mainly how they are produced and how they are processed by those who hear them. This book reveals the physics behind sound creation and details the various properties of sound. It also reveals that the fleshy bits of the human ear, visible on either side of a person's head, are just the tip of the iceberg when it comes to the ear's form and function. Readers are taken on a virtual journey through the human ear for an explanation of how sound is heard. Also discussed is the field of acoustics.

Sound is produced in waves caused by vibrations. The movement of the vibration pushes and pulls air molecules, which crowd together and form invisible ripples in the air. These ripples, called compression waves, travel from the source of the vibration in all directions until they reach a pair of ears, which translate the vibrations into sound.

Strength and frequency (how quickly one complete vibration occurs) each affect how sound is heard. How strong a vibration is determines whether a sound is loud or soft—the stronger it is, the louder. Frequency influences pitch, which is how high or low a sound is.

Sometimes a solid object blocks the path of sound waves traveling through the air. Sound is easily reflected from flat surfaces, meaning that the sound waves reflect off of the object and turn back toward the source. Reflection explains why there is an echo when a person shouts into a canyon that has flat, smooth walls. Reflecting off of curved objects restricts the paths that waves can take, thereby focusing sound as it travels from the source.

The curved shape of part of the outer human ear known as the external auditory meatus, or ear canal, helps focus sound as it is received. Sound waves journey down the ear canal to a membrane called the eardrum. Waves striking the eardrum cause it to vibrate. From there, sound waves travel to the middle ear, where they are passed along a series of three small bones called ossicles and strike another membrane called the round window. Finally, sound moves into the inner ear to the shell-like cochlea, which houses the organ of Corti. Covered in nerve endings that look like tiny hairs, the organ of Corti sends electrical impulses to the brain, where sound is identified.

There are many kinds of sounds, and various ways to interpret those sounds. But, as this book explains, the physics of sound are pretty straightforward—as well as quite interesting.

CHAPTER 1

MAKING SOUND

Every kind of sound is produced by vibration. The sound source may be a violin, an automobile horn, or a barking dog. Whatever it is, some part of it is vibrating while it is producing sound. The vibrations from the source disturb the air in such a way that sound waves are produced. These waves travel out in all directions, expanding in a balloonlike fashion from the source of the sound. If the waves happen to reach someone's ear, they set up vibrations that are perceived as sound.

Sound, then, depends on three things. There must be a vibrating source to set up sound waves, a medium (such as air) to carry the waves, and a receiver to detect them. Sound waves cannot travel through a vacuum.

There is an age-old question concerning the definition of sound. If a tree falls in a forest far from any sound detector (such as a human ear or a microphone), does the tree's crash make any noise? The answer, of course, depends on how sound is defined. If it is thought of as the waves that are carried by the air, the answer is yes—wherever there

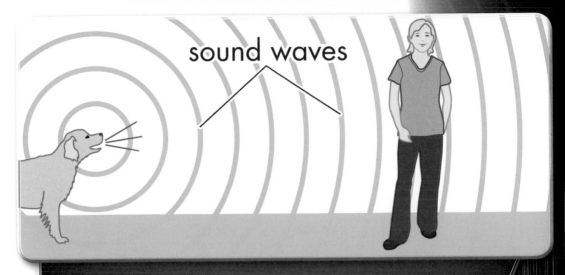

sound waves

Sound waves travel through the air from a source to a receiver.
Encyclopædia Britannica, Inc.

are sound waves there is sound. However, if sound is defined subjectively, as a sensation in the ear, for example, the answer must be no. In that case sound does not exist unless there is a receiver present to detect it. The two definitions are equally correct.

How Sound Is Produced and Carried

It is easy to detect the vibrations of many sources of sound. A radio loudspeaker, for example, vibrates strongly, especially when the volume is turned up. If one lightly touches

Striking a gong initiates vibrations that create a compression sound wave, which travels outward and eventually fades away.
Matthew Wakem/Digital Vision/Getty Images

the speaker cone, one can feel its vibrations as a kind of tickling sensation in the fingertips. If one touches one's throat while singing a low note, one can feel the vibrations of the vocal cords. A common experiment in physics classes is to strike a tuning fork and dip the end of it in water. The vibrating fork splashes the water and sets up little waves that are easy to see.

Sound waves are often compared with water waves but are actually a very different sort of wave. What they are can be seen by considering what happens when an object vibrates in the air. Suppose someone strikes a gong. As the gong vibrates, it alternately bends outward and inward very rapidly. This movement pushes and pulls at the air next to the surface of the metal. Air is made up of tiny molecules, billions of them to every cubic inch or cubic centimeter. Therefore, when the metal gong bends outward, it crowds together those air molecules that are close to its surface. These molecules push outward against other molecules, and they, in turn, push against still others. Thus a compression wave is set into motion. The wave travels outward from the gong, becoming weaker and weaker until it dies away.

A single sound wave such as this does not actually produce a sound, of course. As the gong continues to vibrate, each outward bending of the metal sets up a new compression wave. Between each pair of compression waves is an area in which the molecules of air are spread apart more widely than normal. Such a wave of rarefaction corresponds to a moment in which the gong is bent inward, pulling instead of pushing the molecules. The whole series of compression and rarefaction waves traveling outward from the gong make up what is heard as sound. The sound waves travel in all directions from their source.

REFLECTING AND FOCUSING SOUND WAVES

Like light waves, sound waves can be reflected and focused. An echo is simply a reflection of sound. A flat surface, like that of a cliff or wall, reflects sound better than an irregular surface, which tends to break up sound waves. Echoes are useful in many ways. In a fog, a ship's captain can often tell whether he is near a hilly shoreline by listening for echoes of the ship's whistle. Underwater sonar equipment uses echoes of a supersonic signal similarly to detect submarines. The device automatically

Fireworks exploding over the band shell of the Hollywood Bowl in Los Angeles while an orchestra performs. The curved construction of the shell focuses sound coming from the ampitheater stage. © **AP Images**

times the echo from the submarine's hull and computes the distance. Depth finders use echoes from the ocean bottom to measure the depth of the water.

A band shell focuses the sound of the band in just the same way an automobile headlight reflector focuses light. The headlight reflector and many band shells are in

Speaking into a megaphone intensifies a person's voice. This happens because sound waves are held in and focused in one direction as they are channeled through the walls of the megaphone. **iStockphoto/Thinkstock**

the shape of a parabolic curve. This curve has the property of reflecting spherical waves in such a way that they form a beam. The band shell concentrates the sound on the audience, preventing it from being dissipated in all directions. Spherical surfaces inside buildings may form "whispering galleries." If someone whispers at one spot in such a chamber, he can be clearly heard at another spot yards away.

ECHO

According to Greek myth, a beautiful nymph named Echo fell hopelessly in love with Narcissus, who loved only his own image. She faded away until her voice had only strength enough to whisper the last word of any call she heard.

This was the poetical Greek explanation of an echo. The scientific explanation is that sound waves are reflected from flat surfaces. An irregular surface breaks up the waves, just as a rocky shore breaks water waves into spray. A smooth surface, such as the side of a cliff, reflects sound waves, and the reflection is heard as an echo.

Because the reflected waves have lost strength, they cannot be heard until the original sound has ceased. A person standing about a hundred feet from the reflecting surface can hear only the final syllable of what is called. If the person stands farther back, more and more syllables can be heard.

Sir Isaac Newton used the echo in a corridor at Trinity College, Cambridge, to measure the speed at which sound travels. Standing at one end of the corridor, he started a group of sound waves by stamping his foot. These waves were thrown back by the wall at the far end of the corridor. He knew the distance to the wall and back, and he timed the interval between stamping his foot and hearing the echo. From these factors he calculated a speed for sound that was within a few feet a second of the speed that modern science has determined.

A large pipe organ. Waves from two closely tuned pipes are subject to interference, meaning the waves tend to cancel each other out, producing a beat or quiet pause. haak78/Shutterstock.com

A megaphone and a stethoscope focus sound in different ways. The sides of a megaphone hold the sound waves in and allow them to escape in only one direction, thus intensifying the waves. A stethoscope is a megaphone in reverse. It funnels sound waves from a relatively wide area into a small area.

INTERFERENCE

Sound waves show other properties that resemble those of light. One is the phenomenon called interference. If an identical tone is produced by two sources, the sound waves may get "out of phase"; that is, the compression waves from one source may arrive at the listener's ear along with the rarefaction waves from the other source. If so, they cancel out one another, and no sound is heard.

Interference helps in the formation of sound beats. If two organ pipes, for example, are tuned a few vibrations apart, they produce a throbbing tone when sounded together. If the difference is three vibrations per second, the waves will be out of phase three times in each second and will be in phase an equal number of times. When they are out of phase, there is a moment of comparative silence. When in phase, however, they reinforce each other and increase the intensity of the tone.

CHAPTER 2

THE PROPERTIES OF SOUND

Some sounds are high and others are low. Some are loud while others are barely audible. Sounds can be either pleasant or harsh. The three basic properties of any pure sound are its pitch, its intensity, and its quality.

PITCH

Pitch is simply the rate at which vibrations are produced. This is usually expressed as the number of Hz (hertz, or cycles per second). One cycle is a complete vibration back and forth. The number of Hz is the frequency of the tone. The higher the frequency of a tone, the higher its pitch. When a saxophone is sounding the note A above middle C, the reed in its mouthpiece is vibrating at a frequency of 440 Hz. Twice that frequency (880) gives a note an octave higher; half the frequency (220) produces a note an octave lower.

Another way to define the pitch of a tone is to give its wavelength. The wavelength of a particular tone is equal to the velocity of sound divided by the frequency of the tone. Suppose the frequency is 440. This means that 440 compression waves are formed every second. Since sound travels in air at roughly 1,100 feet (335 meters) a second, the distance between waves is 1,100/440 feet (335/440 meters), or about 212 feet (0.8 meter). This is the wavelength of the tone.

If a source of sound is moving, sound waves are shortened in one direction and lengthened in the opposite. Such shortening and lengthening change the pitch of the tone. This is called the Doppler effect, from the name of the Austrian physicist who first explained it. For instance, when a locomotive is standing still, the sound waves going out from its whistle are evenly spaced. When the locomotive is moving toward an observer, however, the waves bunch together ahead of the source. This causes the pitch of the whistle to rise. Just as the locomotive passes the observer, the pitch of its whistle suddenly drops to a lower tone, for behind the locomotive the sound waves are spread apart.

The Doppler Effect

with locomotive standing still, tone of whistle is normal

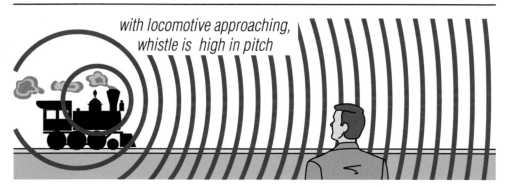

with locomotive approaching, whistle is high in pitch

with locomotive moving away, whistle is low in pitch

Representation of how moving sound creates sound waves of varying length, which affects pitch. Encyclopædia Britannica, Inc.

INTENSITY

The intensity of a sound has nothing to do with its pitch. A high tone can be either loud or soft, and so can a low tone. Intensity depends upon the strength, or amplitude, of the vibrations producing the sound. A piano string, for example, vibrates gently if the key is struck softly. The string swings back and forth in a narrow arc, and the tone it sends out is soft. If the key is struck forcefully, however, the string swings back and forth in a wider arc. The stronger vibration then produces a louder tone.

The explanation of this is that a vibration of greater amplitude compresses the molecules of the air more forcefully and gives them greater energy. When a series of such strong compression waves enters the ear, the brain interprets it as a loud tone. The loudness of sounds is measured in decibels (db). On the scale used, 0 indicates the softest audible sound. The rustle of leaves is rated as 20 db, average street noise as 70, and nearby thunder as 120. Above this level ,sound begins to be painful. Prolonged exposure to sound at such levels may damage hearing.

THE DOPPLER EFFECT

The "Doppler effect" is a term that refers to the apparent difference between the frequency at which sound or light waves leave a source and that at which they reach an observer. The difference is caused by the relative motion of the observer and the wave source. This phenomenon is used in astronomical measurements and in radar and modern navigation. It was first described in 1842 by Austrian physicist Christian Doppler.

The Doppler Shift

The amount of shift depends on the velocity of the object in relationship to the observer: the greater the velocity, the greater the shift.

Absorption lines from an approaching object shift toward the violet (shorter wavelength).

Absorption lines from the sun are used for comparison.

Absorption lines from a receding object shift toward the red (longer wavelength).

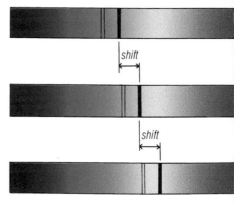

The colored bands are standard spectra. The black lines are absorption lines.

Encyclopædia Britannica, Inc.

The change in pitch of an approaching train horn, mentioned in this section, is an example of the Doppler effect. Similarly, the light from a star, observed from Earth, shifts toward the red end of the spectrum (lower frequency or longer wavelength) if Earth and the star are receding, or moving away from each other, and toward the violet (higher frequency or shorter wavelength) if they are approaching each other. The Doppler effect is used in studying the motion of stars and is an integral part of modern theories of the universe.

SOUND QUALITY

The quality, or timbre, of a sound is more complicated than pitch or intensity. The tone of a flute has a pleasant quality while the screech of a bluejay has an unpleasant one. Neither sound is a simple tone. The flute may be sounding, say, A above middle C. In addition to the frequency of 440 Hz, however, the flute is producing higher frequencies as well. These softer and higher tones are called overtones. In the example of the flute, the main overtones heard are the octave and the 12th. For A, these notes are the next A above and the E above that note. These overtones harmonize well with the principal note (or

The inside of a piano, showing the strings and hammers. Pressing a key softly creates less vibration when the associated hammer hits the string. The result is a quieter note. **Michael Macsuga/Shutterstock.com**

fundamental) and account for the sweet tone of the flute.

Other instruments sound different combinations of overtones, which give them their special tone quality. The human voice and stringed instruments, such as the violin and piano, are very rich in overtones. Overtones that harmonize better than others are notes of the same scale.

THE PRODUCTION OF MUSICAL SOUNDS

There are four classes of musical instruments—string, wind, percussion, and electronic. Each produces tones in a different way. Strings are perhaps simplest to understand.

The pitch of a string depends upon two things—its tension (the pull that is put upon it) and its length. The greater the tension on a string, the higher its pitch. A violin string, practically speaking, is under constant tension. The violinist raises its pitch by shortening the vibrating length of it with the fingers of the hand that is not holding the bow.

When a string is bowed, plucked, or struck near one end, it may vibrate in several ways at once. It vibrates as a whole, sounding the fundamental tone. It may also vibrate in two or more parts at the same time, sounding faintly heard overtones.

Most of the volume of a violin is due to resonance. Without the body of the violin, the strings would produce only very soft tones. The body, however, is constructed to vibrate in sympathy with the strings. Vibrations from a string are transmitted to the body of the instrument. Both the body and the air inside it then vibrate at the same frequency as the string. Because the wood is so much more massive than the string, it sends out more intense sound waves than the string alone can. The tones of piano strings are similarly reinforced by the piano's sounding board.

Sounds thought of as harsh are combinations of tones that do not harmonize. If the raucous call of a bluejay were analyzed, it would be found to be a combination of extremely discordant notes. All noises are miscellaneous combinations of tones, unpleasant because they are unrelated.

THE SPEED OF SOUND

Sound waves travel at a constant speed, regardless of the loudness or softness of a sound. Temperature, however, does affect their speed. At room temperature (70° F, or 22.2° C), sound travels in air at a speed of 1,129 feet (344 meters) per second. With each rise of one degree Fahrenheit, the speed increases by more than one foot per second. (With each rise of one degree Celsius, the speed increases by about 0.6 meter per second.) Air pressure has little or no effect. Humidity has a slight effect, the

A woman playing a violin. The body of the violin is designed to make the sound produced by the strings resonate. Andrii Muzyka/ Shutterstock.com

speed of sound being somewhat greater in humid air than in dry air. Since 1,129 feet is about one–fifth of a mile, sound waves travel one mile in about five seconds (or one kilometer in about three seconds). Thus one can

A blue jay, singing while perched on a tree stump. The bird's call is made up of discordant notes, or notes that don't blend or harmonize well. **Steve Byland/Shutterstock.com**

tell about how many miles away lightning is by counting the seconds between its flash and the thunder and dividing by five. (To determine the approximate distance in kilometers, divide by three instead.)

The speed of light is faster than the speed of sound. Therefore, people see lightning flash from miles away before hearing the thunder that accompanies it during a storm. **Stockbyte/Thinkstock**

A woman testing speakers in a padded, soundproof room. Certain materials, such as rubber and foam, absorb sound. Ridges and channels in the material also help with absorption.
David Joel/Photographer's Choice/Getty Images

Many other substances are better conductors of sound than air. Like all gases, air is a poor medium for sound waves. Liquids, such as water, are better, and rigid solid substances, such as iron and stone, are best of all. Sound waves travel in much the same way in liquids and solids as in air. The molecules of a liquid move about less freely than do molecules of a gas, and the molecules of a solid less freely still. Compression waves, however, are formed and transmitted in them just as in air. In a good conductor, sound not only travels faster, but also travels farther before it dies away.

A few solids are much poorer conductors of sound than air. Rubber, cork, cotton, and felt, for example, tend to absorb sound waves rather than transmit them. For that reason, such substances are often used for soundproofing to deaden unwanted noises.

CHAPTER 8

HOW SOUND IS PROCESSED

Vibrations of air molecules moving through the air are received and translated into messages that the brain recognizes as sound by a complex organ—the ear. The ear has two important, but different, functions: hearing sound and sensing the body's equilibrium, or balance. The mechanisms for these processes are located within a hollow space in the skull's temporal bone.

THE HUMAN EAR

The ear has three separate sections—the outer ear, the middle ear, and the inner ear. Each section performs a specific function, related to either hearing or balance.

PARTS OF THE EAR

The three parts of the outer ear are the auricle (also called the pinna), the external

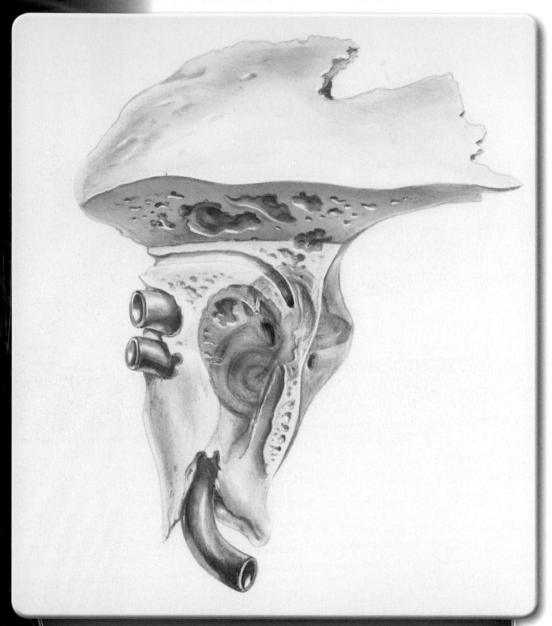

Illustration of a human skull, showing a portion of the temporal bone. The mechanisms of the ear are housed in the temporal bone, a hollow space at the base of the skull. **DEA Picture Library/Getty Images**

auditory meatus (or ear canal), and the tympanic membrane (or eardrum). The pinna collects sound waves from the air. It funnels them into a channel-like tube, the external auditory meatus. This is a curved corridor that leads to the tympanic membrane. The eardrum separates the external ear from the middle ear. The middle ear is an irregular-shaped, air-filled space, about 0.75 inch (1.9 centimeters) high and 0.2 inch (0.5 centimeter) wide. A chainlike link of three tiny bones, the ossicles, spans the middle ear.

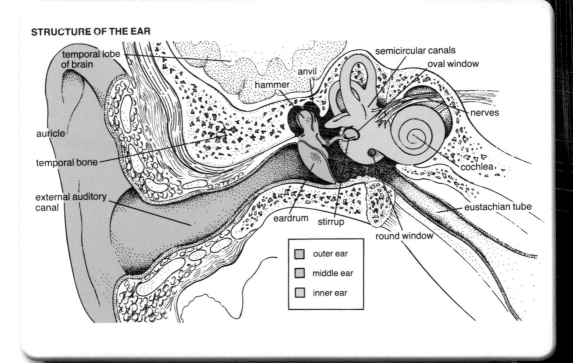

STRUCTURE OF THE EAR

Structure of the ear. Encyclopædia Britannica, Inc.

When sound waves strike the outer surface of the eardrum, it vibrates. These vibrations are mechanically transmitted through the middle ear by the ossicles.

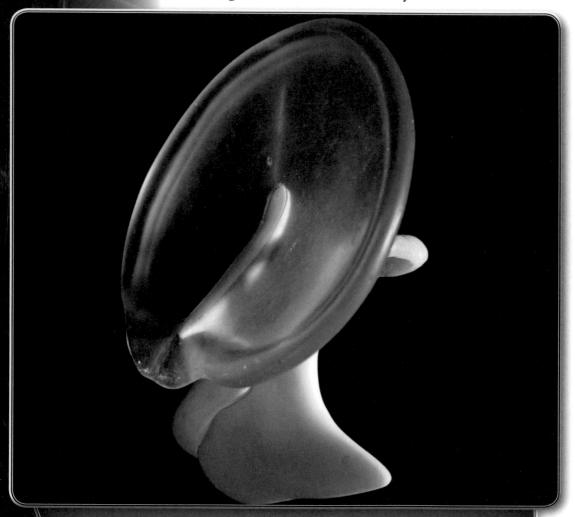

A model of the human eardrum, showing the bones by which sound is transmitted, called the ossicles. **Ralph Hutchings/Visuals Unlimited/Getty Images**

The malleus, or hammer, is the first ossicle to receive vibrations from the eardrum. It passes them to the second ossicle—the incus, or anvil. The third ossicle—the stapes, or stirrup—relays the vibrations to a membrane that covers the opening into the inner ear. This opening is the round window.

Like the eardrum, the round window's membrane transmits vibrations. It directs vibrations into the inner ear, where they enter a fluid that fills a structure called the cochlea. This is a coiled tube that resembles a snail's shell. If the cochlea were straightened out, it would measure slightly more than 1 inch (2.54 centimeters).

Within the cochlea is housed the true mechanism of hearing, called the organ of Corti. It contains tiny hairlike nerve endings anchored in a basilar membrane, which extends throughout the cochlea. The unattached tips of these nerve endings are in contact with an overhanging "roof membrane," called the tectorial membrane.

When vibrations pass into the inner ear, they cause waves to form in the cochlear fluid. Receptor nerve cells in the organ of Corti are highly sensitive to these waves. Other specialized nerve cells send the electrochemical impulses produced by the wave motion into the cochlear branch of the acoustic nerve. This nerve carries the impulses to the brain, where sound is identified.

Diseases and damage

Each of the ear's three sections can be affected by diseases that relate to the structure, tissues, and function of that particular part of the ear. Diseases of the outer ear affect the skin, cartilage, and the glands and hair follicles in the outer ear canal. The sound-transmitting function of the outer ear is damaged when the ear canal becomes filled with a tumor, earwax, or infected material. When these conditions occur, sound cannot reach the eardrum.

There are several common diseases of the outer ear. Frostbite is a condition in which the exposed part of the ear becomes frozen and numb, resulting in a temporary loss of skin sensation. An injury that causes bleeding between the cartilage and the skin may produce a hematoma, which is a smooth, rounded, non-tender, purplish swelling. External otitis is an infection of the outer ear canal caused by molds or microorganisms. It occurs most often in warm humid climates and among swimmers. A greenish

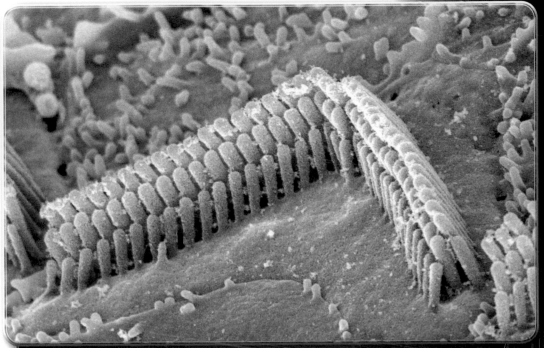

A colorized micrograph of organ of Corti nerve endings. These structures mark the starting point of a series of electrochemical impulses that are recognized by the brain as sound. Dr. David Furness, Keele University/Science Photo Library/Getty Images

or brownish, musty, foul-smelling discharge develops in the outer ear canal, and the outer ear becomes tender, red, and much thicker than usual.

A common middle ear infection is secretory otitis media, in which the middle-ear cavity becomes filled with a clear, pale-yellowish, noninfected fluid. This develops when not enough air comes into the

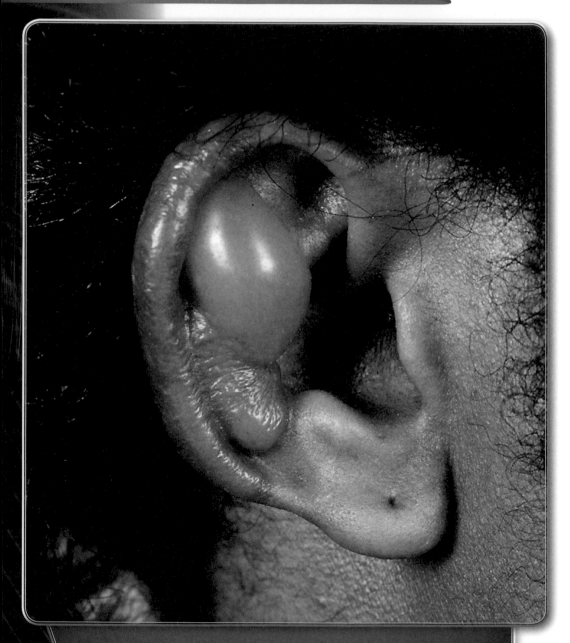

An image depicting the damage frostbite can inflict on the human ear. © **J.Barabe/Custom Medical Stock Photo**

cavity from the eustachian tube. A painless impairment of hearing results. Head colds, allergic reactions of the membranes of the eustachian tube, and an enlarged adenoid are common causes of this condition.

A common inner-ear disease is congenital nerve deafness, which is caused by a defect of the hearing nerves in the cochlea. This may be present at birth or develop during or soon after birth. Usually both inner ears are affected to a similar degree. A severe impairment of hearing generally occurs but not always.

Ototoxic, or ear-poisoning, drugs can cause temporary and even permanent damage to the hearing-nerve function. Large doses of such salicylates as aspirin may cause ringing in the ears of some persons, followed by a temporary decrease in hearing. When a person stops taking the drug, hearing returns to normal. Certain antibiotics may cause permanent damage to the hearing-nerve function.

Exposure to various degrees of noise may cause temporary or permanent hearing damage. A single exposure to such an extremely intense sound as an explosion may produce a severe and permanent loss of hearing. Repeated exposures to sounds that reach

Australian rugby player Adam Dykes displays an ear hematoma resulting from an injury during a game in 2007. Bleeding under the skin is responsible for the discoloration and swelling. **Mark Nolan/Getty Images**

more than 80 to 90 decibels may cause gradual loss of hearing. This happens because the hair cells of the inner ear, and sometimes even the nerve fibers, may be destroyed. The levels of noise produced by rock music bands are frequently more than 110 decibels. In the United

A member of an airline's ground crew, wearing earphones to protect his hearing. High-decibel noise, like that from an aircraft, can severely damage the ear's mechanisms. **Siri Stafford/Stone/Getty Images**

States, there are laws that require workers who are exposed to sound levels higher than 90 decibels to wear some form of protection. Earplugs or earmuffs are often used.

DECIBEL

A decibel is a unit for measuring the loudness of sounds to normal human ears. A related unit is the bel (1 bel equals 10 decibels).

Because it requires about a tenfold increase in power for a sound to register twice as loud to the human ear, a logarithmic scale is useful for comparing sound intensity. Thus, the threshold of human hearing (the softest audible sound) is assigned the value of 0 decibels. Each increase of 10 decibels corresponds to a tenfold increase in intensity and a doubling in loudness. The "threshold of pain" for intensity varies from 120 to 130 decibels among different individuals. In practice, measurements are made with a special sound meter (acoustimeter) containing numerous electrical circuits whose aggregate sensitivity to pitch and loudness correspond to that of the human ear.

THE ABILITY TO HEAR SOUND

The human ear cannot hear all possible frequencies. Very few people can hear any fewer than 16 Hz or any more than about 20 kHz (kilohertz—1 kHz equals 1,000 Hz). Music rarely makes use of this whole range of audible frequencies. The lowest note on a piano has a frequency of 27 Hz and the highest note a little more than 4 kHz. Frequency-modulation (FM) radio stations broadcast notes up to 15 kHz.

Frequencies greater than the human ear can hear are called supersonic or ultrasonic waves. A silent dog whistle is pitched at supersonic frequency. A dog hears these waves as sound, though a human being does not. Extremely high frequencies of 100 to 500 kHz can cause strong physical and chemical reactions. They can force water and oil to emulsify, dust to collect, and gases held in liquids or molten metals to bubble out. They destroy certain types of bacteria.

HEARING LOSS

The outer ears are the most noticeable portion of a human's hearing apparatus, but the most important hearing parts—the mechanical and neural components—are within the skull. Damage to either set of components, or to both, can result in a loss of hearing that may be partial or complete. The word "deafness" is used to describe any degree of hearing loss, though it is most commonly used where there is a total inability to hear.

Two major categories of hearing loss are recognized: conduction deafness and nerve deafness. Conduction deafness is caused by any obstruction to the sound-conducting mechanism of the outer or middle ear that prevents sound waves from reaching the inner ear. Nerve deafness results from a loss of function of the sensory apparatus of the inner ear or its connecting nerve pathways to the cortex of the brain.

Hearing loss in infants may be caused by heredity or infection. In loss due to heredity, the child usually inherits a failure in the development in the nerve components of the ear. In some cases, however, inherited deformities result in the partial or complete closure of the external canal or the middle ear. Some hearing problems in babies are caused by infection of the mother during pregnancy. Rubella (German measles), chicken pox, and other diseases, when contracted by a pregnant woman, can cause damage to the developing inner ears of the fetus. Infants who get viral infections during the first year may also develop hearing loss.

In children, a common cause of hearing impairment is inflammation of the middle ear, or otitis media, often due to infection. Hearing loss associated with otitis media is usually temporary.

The most frequent cause of deafness in persons between the ages of 20 and 50 is a condition called otosclerosis, in which new bone growth in the middle ear blocks off the passage of sound waves and exposure to noise. Prolonged exposure to loud noise or a single exposure to extremely loud noise can damage the delicate structures and nerves of the inner ear.

People tend to lose some of their hearing gradually with advancing age. This type of hearing loss, called presbycusis, is the natural result of a variety of problems associated with aging.

HEARING RESTORATION AND AID

Surgery can restore at least some hearing in most individuals with conduction deafness, but it is not an option for those with nerve

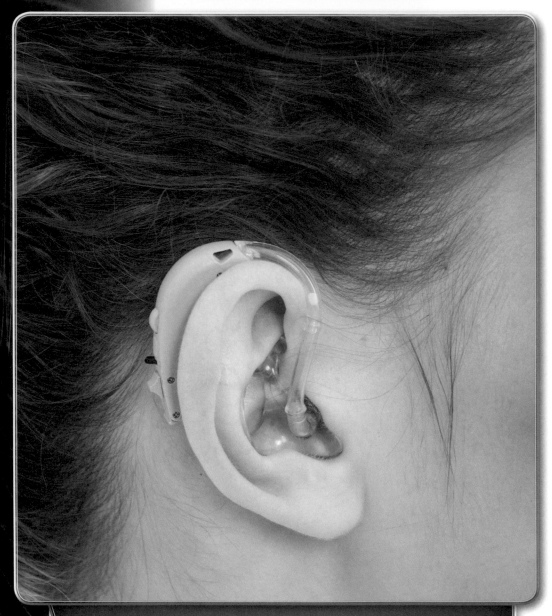

Most hearing aids, such as the one worn by the woman in this picture, are worn outside the ear, with a portion that fits into the ear canal. Piotr Marcinski/Shutterstock.com

deafness. The objectives of surgery may be to open the outer ear canal if it is blocked, to repair or replace damaged eardrum membranes, or to eliminate chronic infection. In other cases, surgery may reestablish a connection between the chain of tiny bones that carry sound vibrations from the eardrum to the inner ear.

Many people with hearing loss retain some ability to hear. Devices that amplify sounds, or make them louder, can help optimize this residual hearing, though they cannot restore normal hearing. The most common are hearing aids, which are electromechanical, battery-operated devices that increase the loudness of sounds. They may help people of all ages with mild to extreme conduction or nerve deafness. Most styles are attached to the outer ear or inserted into the ear canal. All hearing aids have three basic parts: a microphone to receive sound waves and convert them into electrical current, an amplifier to make the current stronger, and an earphone to convert the stronger current back into sound waves.

In the late 20th century, cochlear implants were introduced as an aid for people with severe to complete hearing loss. The cochlea, a coiled, fluid-filled organ in the inner ear,

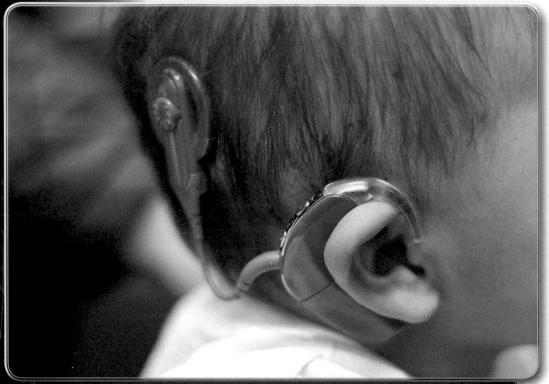

A young boy fitted with a cochlear implant getting his hearing tested. The outer portion of the device sends signals to the implant, which is surgically placed deep inside the patient's ear. © **AP Images**

contains the sensory organ of hearing. In individuals with normal hearing, the cochlea responds to sound vibrations from the middle ear by triggering nerve impulses that travel to the brain, which interprets them as sound. A cochlear implant consists of a synthetic cochlea made of tiny wires that is surgically implanted in the inner ear. The implant is connected to a plug inserted under the skin behind the ear. The plug, in turn, is connected to an external microphone attached to a small microprocessor that can be worn on a belt or carried.

The synthetic cochlea converts sound waves into electrical signals that it transmits to the brain. After intensive postoperative training, many people who receive an implant learn to interpret those electrical signals as sound. Although a cochlear implant cannot provide a normal sense of hearing, it can help some deaf people perceive sound in their environment and communicate with spoken language. The implants seem to be most effective in young children and in adults who lost their hearing after they learned to speak.

CHAPTER 4

THE FIELD OF ACOUSTICS

What do these seemingly unrelated experts have in common: the scientist studying the transmission of sound under water, the physician using ultrasonics to study the condition of an unborn child, the engineer developing techniques for quieting a noisy truck or providing good listening conditions for a concert hall, and the audiologist evaluating the hearing of a patient? All are involved in the interdisciplinary science called acoustics, a science that deals with the production, control, transmission, reception, and effects of sound. In 1964 the prominent physicist R. Bruce Lindsay published what would come to be known as Lindsay's wheel of acoustics, an outline of the field in which he demonstrated that acoustics has applications in the life sciences, the earth sciences, engineering, and the arts.

An audiologist checking a young woman's hearing. Spencer Grant/Photo Researchers/Getty Images

NOISE CONTROL MODEL

The acoustical engineer is called upon to study such everyday problems as the reduction of noises produced by truck tires, garbage disposals, microwave ovens, office copying machines, and dentists' drills. In

55

An acoustical engineer setting up a product sound test in France.
Pierre Bessard/REA/Redux

attempting to solve these problems, the engineer often utilizes noise control models. The models include the sources of the noise, how the noise is transmitted to the receivers, and the identity of the receivers.

In controlling a noise problem, the acoustician may elect to reduce the noise generated by the sources or to modify the path that is traveled by the noise, such as by installing a partial barrier. Another method would be to protect the receivers by providing hearing protection devices.

ARCHITECTURAL ACOUSTICS

An area of acoustics that is often misunderstood is that of architectural acoustics. It is generally appreciated that good acoustics are

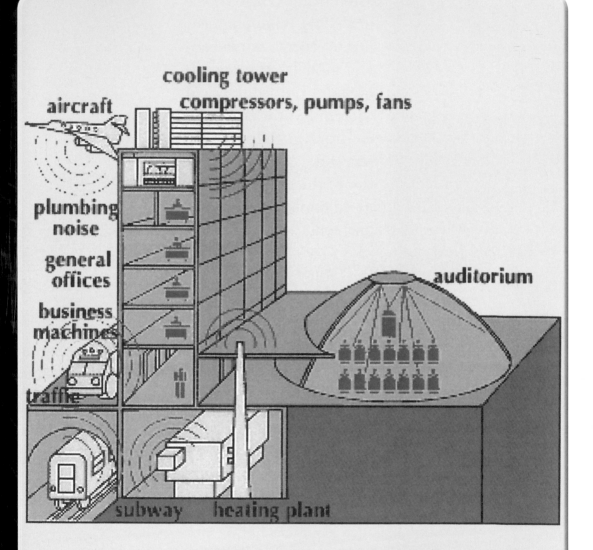

A diagram illustrates factors in architectural acoustics. Noise sources, acoustic radiation characteristics, and treatment options must all be considered. **Encyclopædia Britannica, Inc.**

important in the design of concert halls, radio and television studios, and structures for similar purposes. However, when it comes to designing classrooms, shopping center malls, apartment complexes, or general home and office environments, acoustical considerations are often neglected.

Those involved in planning areas to be used by people should consider a host of factors, including the intended use of the area, the types of people who will use it, and many others. Failure to consider principles of good acoustics during the initial design and construction of an area usually results in environments where individuals cannot function optimally. Correcting a bad acoustical design after the completion of a project often costs many times more than having done the job correctly in the first place.

ULTRASONICS

Acoustic signals are often used to detect objects inside solid matter, such as impurities in metals, or objects hidden under liquids, such as those submerged in an ocean. Such detection and identification of objects hidden from the eye is one application of ultrasonics. Ultrasonic waves, or sounds at

The bumper of a bus equipped with an ultrasonic sensor (under the turn signal). The sensors are designed to detect objects at a distance using sound waves, which may help drivers avoid crashes. **Stefan Zaklin/Getty Images**

a pitch much higher than can be heard by the human ear, are also of major importance in medicine. They are used to study internal organs, assess the condition of an unborn child, and detect foreign objects for removal from the body.

The instruments used both send out waves and receive those reflected by an object encountered. This technique is also utilized in submarines to locate objects in the ocean and by engineers in designing robots for undersea detection work.

STRESS TESTING

Another application of acoustic technology concerns the nondestructive evaluation of critical components of machinery. The continuous reliability of materials in, for instance, jet engines, automotive gas turbines, or nuclear steam generators is critical from both safety and performance standpoints. To ensure reliable performance, it is necessary to use techniques that allow the evaluation of the components while the systems are in actual use. One such technique uses acoustic emissions produced by components as they are stressed during the operation of the equipment. As a turbine blade, shaft, or

THE USE OF ULTRASOUND IN MEDICINE

In medicine, the use of high-frequency sound (ultrasonic) waves to produce images of structures within the human body is known as ultrasound. Ultrasonic waves are sound waves that are above the range of sound audible to humans. The ultrasonic waves are produced by the electrical stimulation of a piezoelectric crystal and can be aimed at a specific area of the body. (Piezolectric crystals are crystals that generate an electric charge when they are purposefully misshapen.) As the waves travel through bodily tissues, they are reflected back at any point where there is a change in tissue density, as, for instance, in the border between two different organs of the body. The reflected echoes are received by an electronic apparatus that determines the intensity level of the echoes and the position of the tissue giving rise to the echoes. The images thus formed can be displayed in static form, or, through the use of rapid multiple sound scans, they can in effect provide a moving picture of the inside of the body.

Part of ultrasound's usefulness derives from the fact that the sound waves are less potentially harmful to human tissues than are X-rays or other ionizing radiations.

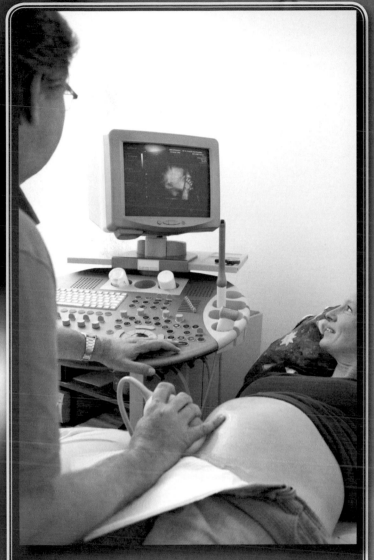

A technician performing an ultrasound exam on a pregnant woman. Ultrasonic waves reflected off various tissue densities give trained medical workers an accurate picture of what's happening inside the human body. Schweinepriester/Shutterstock.com

Ultrasound is most commonly used to examine fetuses in utero in order to ascertain size, position, or abnormalities. Ultrasound is also used to provide images of the heart, the liver, the kidneys, the gallbladder, the breasts, the eyes, and major blood vessels. It also can be used to diagnose tumors and to guide certain procedures, such as needle biopsies, the introduction of tubes for drainage, and intra-uterine corrective surgery.

Images produced by ultrasound are not as precise as images obtained through computerized axial tomography (CAT) or magnetic resonance imaging (MRI). However, ultrasound is used in many procedures because it is quick and relatively inexpensive and has no known biological hazards when used within the diagnostic range.

Research has indicated that ultrasound may also be used as a form of treatment. For example, low-intensity pulsed ultrasound can facilitate healing in certain types of bone fractures, including stress fractures and delayed union fractures, the latter of which take an unusually long time to heal.

other component is strained, it produces its own characteristic acoustic signature pattern that may be used for identification purposes. (The procedure is similar to that of using voice patterns for the purpose of identifying individuals.) If the component begins to fail, its acoustic signature will change. The detection of such a change may serve as a warning for the replacement of the component before it causes failure of the entire piece of equipment.

COMMUNICATION

The areas of speech and hearing are also part of the field of acoustics. When one walks beside a busy road and something unusual happens, for instance, the first indication may come from hearing a different or sudden sound. This ability to perceive acoustical warnings from a specific direction is essential for survival.

The ability to communicate by spoken language is unique to humans, and is frequently utilized every day. How many times a day does one pick up the telephone to obtain information about an assignment, to make a date, or to check on a new movie? The individual placing the phone call, the telephone system that transmits the spoken information, the environments where the caller and receiver are each located, and the individual on the receiving end all form a complex system. Acoustical scientists are deeply involved in studying this system in attempting to improve communication.

Conclusion

Much of what is known about the world was learned through sight and hearing. The ancients naturally were interested in light and sound. Yet of these two, sound was much easier to understand, and people began discovering facts about sound at an early date.

Humans' love of music led them to build musical instruments from which they learned that all bodies that produce sounds are vibrating. Faster vibrations produce sound of higher pitch, and slower vibrations produce a lower pitch. The ancient Greek mathematician Pythagoras—generally regarded as the founder of acoustics—investigated the laws of stringed instruments in the 6th century BCE. Some 500 years later Vitruvius, a Roman architectural engineer, wrote that sound is produced in the form of concentric waves like those made by a stone when it is thrown into still water. Today, it is known that sound waves consist of an ever-widening sphere of compressions, regions where the air molecules are crowded together and that these compressions are separated by rarefactions, regions where the molecules are farther apart than usual.

The wide-ranging field of acoustics has grown to have important applications in almost every area of life. It has been fundamental to many developments in the arts—some of which, especially in the area of musical scales and instruments, took place after long experimentation by artists and were only much later explained as theory by scientists. For example, much of what is now known about architectural acoustics was actually learned by trial and error over centuries of experience and has only recently been formalized into a science.

Other applications of acoustic technology are in the study of geologic, atmospheric, and underwater phenomena. Psychoacoustics, the study of the physical effects of sound on biological systems, has been of interest since Pythagoras's time, but the application of modern ultrasonic technology has only recently provided some of the most exciting developments in medicine. Even today, research continues into many aspects of the fundamental physical processes involved in waves and sound, as well as possible applications of these processes in modern life.

acoustic Relating to the sense or organs of hearing, to sound, or to the science of sounds.

amplitude The extent of a vibratory movement (as of a sound wave) measured from the mean position to an extreme.

audible Capable of being heard.

cochlear Of or pertaining to a coiled-tube structure of the inner ear.

compression wave A wave created by a series of air molecules that push outward against one another from a source point.

conduction The transmission of energy (as sound) through a stable, non-moving medium or material.

decibel A unit for expressing the relative intensity of sounds.

Doppler effect The apparent difference between the frequency at which sound or light waves leave a source and that at which they reach an observer.

frequency The number of complete oscillations per second of energy (as sound) in the form of waves.

intensity The magnitude of a energy force, such as sound waves, per unit.

interference The mutual effect on the meeting of two wave trains that creates areas of increased and decreased amplitude (louder and softer sound).

modulation An inflection of the tone or pitch of a sound.

ossicle A small bone or bony structure.

otitis An inflammation of the ear.

overtone When a higher tone is produced at the same time as a fundamental tone; taken together, the two tones create harmony.

pitch The highness or lowness of sound (especially a musical tone), determined by the frequency of the waves producing it.

rarefaction A region where the molecules in sound waves are farther apart than usual.

reflection The return of sound (or light) waves from a surface.

resonance A quality imparted to sound by increased vibration.

temporal Bodily part (as a bone or muscle) that is near the temples or the sides of the skull behind the eye sockets.

timbre The resonance by which the ear recognizes and identifies; the quality of sound.

tone A sound of definite pitch and vibration.

tympanic Of or relating to a thin tense membrane covering within the middle ear.

ultrasound Pertaining to the use of waves and vibrations at a pitch much higher than can be heard by the human ear to detect objects through solid matter.

wavelength The distance between the crest of a wave, such as a sound wave.

Acoustical Society of America
Suite 1NO1
2 Huntington Quadrangle
Melville, NY 11747-4502
(516)-576-2360
Web site: http://acousticalsociety.org
The Acoustical Society of America is an
international scientific organization that
strives to share information regarding the
field of acoustics. Among other efforts,
the group offers educational outreach
programs and publications.

American Academy of Audiology
11730 Plaza America Drive, Suite 300
Reston, VA 20190
(800) 222-2336
Web site: http://www.audiology.org
The American Academy of Audiology is
an organization that offers its members
professional development, education,
and research opportunities. The
organization also strives to increase
public awareness of hearing and balance
disorders.

American Institute of Physics (AIP)
One Physics Ellipse

College Park, MD 20740

(301) 209-3100

Web site: http://www.aip.org

The members of the AIP include scientists,
engineers, and educators who seek to
share knowledge within the physics
community and promote the study of
physics to the public through programs,
publications, and outreach services.

Audio Engineering Society, Inc.

60 East 42nd Street, Room 2520

New York, NY 10165-2520

(212) 661-0477

Web site: http://www.aes.org

The Audio Engineering Society is an international professional organization that
promotes advances in audio technology
and processes.

Canadian Acoustical Association (CAA)

P.O. Box 74068

Ottawa, ON K1M 2H9

Canada

(613) 562-5800

Web site: http://caa-aca.ca

The CAA is a national professional organization dedicated to the growth and

practical application of knowledge pertaining to acoustics through education and research.

Canadian Association of Physicists (CAP)
Suite 112, MacDonald Building
University of Ottawa
150 Louis Pasteur Priv.
Ottawa, ON K1N 6N5
Canada
(613) 562-5614
Web site: http://www.cap.ca
Committed to advancing research and education in the field of physics, the CAP sponsors meetings for physicists from throughout Canada, provides lectures and resources for students pursuing physics-related careers, and promotes the importance of physics to the public at large.

National Science Foundation (NSF)
4201 Wilson Boulevard
Arlington, VA 22230
(703) 292-5111
Web site: http://www.nsf.gov
The NSF supports scientific research and advancement throughout the United

States in a variety of fields, including physics and other physical sciences.

WEB SITES

Due to the changing nature of Internet links, Rosen Educational Services has developed an online list of Web sites related to the subject of this book. This site is updated regularly. Please use this link to access the list:

http://www.rosenlinks.com/inphy/sound

Bibliography

Brooks, Christopher N. *Architectural Acoustics* (McFarland & Co., 2003).

Coulter, George, and Coulter, Shirley. *Science in Music* (Rourke Publications, 1995).

Crocker, Malcolm J., ed. *Encyclopedia of Acoustics* (John Wiley, 1997).

Everest, F. Alton. *The Master Handbook of Acoustics* (McGraw-Hill, 2001).

Farndon, John. *Sound and Hearing* (Benchmark Books, 2001).

Goldsmith, Mike. *Light and Sound* (Kingfisher, 2009).

Kruth, Patricia, and Stobart, Henry. *Sound* (Cambridge University Press, 2007).

Levine, Shar, and Johnstone, Leslie. *The Science of Sound and Music* (Sterling Publishing, 2000).

Sherman, Josepha. *The Ear: Learning How We Hear* (Rosen Publishing Group, 2002).

Trumbauer, Lisa. *All About Sound* (Children's Press, 2004.)